APPEARANCE ANXIETY

APPEARANCE ANXIETY

A GUIDE TO UNDERSTANDING BODY
DYSMORPHIC DISORDER FOR YOUNG
PEOPLE, FAMILIES AND PROFESSIONALS

National and Specialist OCD, BDD and
Related Disorders Service for Young People,
Maudsley Hospital

Jessica Kingsley *Publishers*
London and Philadelphia

First published in 2019
by Jessica Kingsley Publishers
73 Collier Street
London N1 9BE, UK
and
400 Market Street, Suite 400
Philadelphia, PA 19106, USA

www.jkp.com

Library of Congress Cataloging in Publication Data
Names: Jassi, Amita, author.
Title: Appearance anxiety : a guide to understanding body dysmorphic disorder
for young people, families and professionals / Amita Jassi, National and
Specialist OCD, BDD and Related Disorders Service, Maudsley Hospital.
Description: London ; Philadelphia : Jessica Kingsley Publishers, 2018.
Identifiers: LCCN 2018039328 | ISBN 9781785924569
Subjects: LCSH: Body dysmorphic disorder--Juvenile literature.
Classification: LCC RC569.5.B64 J37 2018 | DDC 616.85/200835--
dc23 LC record available at https://lccn.loc.gov/2018039328

British Library Cataloguing in Publication Data
A CIP catalogue record for this book is available from the British Library

ISBN 978 1 78592 456 9
eISBN 978 1 78450 832 6

Printed and bound in Great Britain

MIX
Paper from
responsible sources
FSC® C013056

CONTENTS

CONTRIBUTORS

(in alphabetical order)

Emma Beardsworth

Laura Bowyer

Emily Brookes

Robbie Burton

Bruce Clark

Rory Daniels

Amita Jassi

Georgina Krebs

Angela Lewis

Elias Marchetti

Benedetta Monzani

Lauren Peile

Katie Holland Whitehead

PREFACE

In our specialist body dysmorphic disorder (BDD) service, time and time again we have given a diagnosis of BDD and offered as much information as we could, yet we always felt there was something missing. We wanted to give young people and their families something to take away with them – a source of information to answer the hundreds of questions that would inevitably run through their minds once they left the clinic. Families often asked us for information they could share with others, in an easy-to-read and accessible format. Clinicians and other professionals frequently contacted us, asking for resources to aid their understanding of BDD. Additionally, we were aware there was a need to provide information to young people who were unsure if BDD was an explanation for their difficulties, and to support them in considering this diagnosis as a possibility. We searched and soon realised there was no such resource available. This was the inspiration behind us pulling together our knowledge and experience to write this book. This is the first book to be written on BDD for young people, their families and professionals.

BDD is a common yet under-recognised and devastating disorder. Looking back over our years working in mental health, we realise that in the past we had often missed this issue. Not only can BDD be missed altogether, but it is often misdiagnosed or mistreated, which can have a major impact on the lives of young people and families. Writing this book is part of our mission to increase awareness and understanding of BDD to stop this from happening. It is important that people are able to spot BDD and understand the condition, in order to access the right support. We know that with evidence-based treatment specifically for BDD, people can recover.

This book aims to take readers on a journey from the point of recognising BDD through to treatment, as well as offering practical guidelines on what families and professionals can do to help. This book also addresses questions about causes, the influence of social media and the outcomes of cosmetic procedures. We cover a lot of ground in this book but have tried to keep it short and to the point. We have written it without jargon and in the way we convey this information to people we see in our clinic.

We would like to thank all the young people and the families we work with for their inspiration and advice in preparing this book. Also, without the thoughtful advice and input from our colleagues, this book would never have been possible.

Dr Amita Jassi
Consultant Clinical Psychologist and Lead for BDD service National and
Specialist OCD, BDD and Related Disorders Service for Young People,
Maudsley Hospital, South London and Maudsley NHS Trust

Dr Bruce Clark
Consultant Child and Adolescent Psychiatrist National and Specialist OCD,
BDD and Related Disorders Service for Young People, Maudsley Hospital and
Clinical Director for CAMHS, South London and Maudsley NHS Trust

A MESSAGE FROM A YOUNG PERSON WITH BDD

My name is Emily, I'm 18 years old and I have BDD. My BDD meant I constantly looked in the mirror, spent hours doing my make-up and getting ready. I would think about my appearance and how ugly I thought I was for most of the day. It affected my day-to-day life; I refused to attend school and I would make up excuses so I didn't have to socialise with friends. Looking back, I realise the negative effect social media had on my illness. I would compare myself to unrealistic Photoshopped images of celebrities and models. In addition, I was obsessed with Googling plastic surgery procedures and beauty treatments that I thought would help my self-esteem. I would take lots of 'selfies' and edit them to make them look acceptable to me.

BDD has robbed me of my teenage years; I missed out on three years of my education, resulting in me having no qualifications. I wasn't able to go to prom or go on school trips, nor did I go to friends' birthdays or parties.

What saddens me the most is that I missed out on several Christmas gatherings and holidays abroad with my family.

The diagnosis of my illness was not quick or straight-forward. I was originally referred to services when I was 12 years old. My anxiety levels had risen considerably when I moved to secondary school and I felt out of place and judged by my peers. I attended weekly therapy sessions and tried multiple drugs at various doses to try to find one that worked best for me. I completed a variety of tests to rule out autism and personality disorders. Eventually, I became disillusioned and tired of talking about my anxiety and frequently refused to attend. What was missing was a diagnosis and a pathway to recovery.

At the age of 13, desperate to wrestle some control back into my life, I turned to anorexia and found myself in a specialist clinic for six months. I was eventually discharged, having fully recovered from my eating disorder but still carrying my underlying issues of BDD. What followed was three years of anger, rebellion, depression and self-harm.

Although I had been receiving counselling and treatment for anxiety, it was five years before I was diagnosed with BDD. I was referred to the Maudsley in January 2016 and was eventually assessed in May 2016 and started treatment with them. At first, I was sceptical and didn't think the treatment would help. I thought it would be another random person with little understanding that I had to explain my whole life to. I was fed up and unoptimistic. I had already participated in CBT therapy, so I knew what to expect and how treatment would be challenging.

Maudsley is in London, which was an hour-and-a-half commute, so that in itself was a challenge. My first few sessions at Maudsley were eye-opening. I finally had someone who understood me and who could empathise with me. I felt like I had really connected with my therapist. We would laugh in our sessions and I actually enjoyed her company. However, it wasn't all fun. Having to physically challenge my thoughts and inhibitions was hard and mentally draining, but it was also very rewarding.

My advice to anyone going through this treatment is to go in with an open mind and to have that motivation to want to get better. I also think it's very important that you get along with your therapist and you feel like you can tell them anything. You will inevitably have blips, but this is normal and part of recovery.

I'm now 18, and I have reconnected with my friends. We regularly go out, and I am now starting to enjoy my teenage years. It's fair to say that there is no magic wand and I still have my anxiety, but I have learnt to cope with it better. The coping mechanisms that help me are learning to put less pressure on myself and being more comfortable in my skin. In therapy, you are given lots of coping strategies, and the secret is to work out which ones work best for you.

I wish you all the best in your treatment; remember to stay positive and optimistic. There is a way to recover and cope with anxiety and BDD, and you can ultimately lead a relatively normal life and find happiness.

Emily Brookes

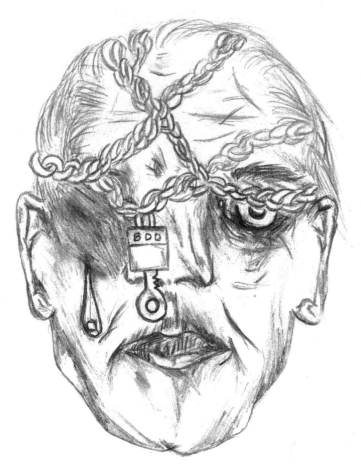

Rory Daniels

1

WHAT IS BDD AND DO I HAVE IT?

This chapter will tell you:

- what BDD is and how it differs from normal appearance concerns

- the common worries associated with BDD

- the common behaviours associated with BDD

- how BDD differs from eating disorders

- what muscle dysmorphia is

- how to figure out whether or not you have BDD.

The fact that you are reading this book means that you are probably struggling with worries about your appearance or you know somebody who is. You might be thinking, 'But isn't it normal to worry about the way you look?' Well, you would be right! Virtually everybody worries about their appearance from time to time, especially during teenage years, and that is not necessarily a problem. However, for some young people these worries snowball. Appearance worries can get to a level where they take over a young person's life, make them feel miserable and get in the way of everyday activities. If this has happened to you, it is worth considering whether you have body dysmorphic disorder (BDD).

What is body dysmorphic disorder?

The core feature of BDD is worrying about perceived flaws in appearance. The flaws are things that other people cannot see or do not generally notice. For example, a young person with BDD may spend hours every day worrying that their nose is crooked, when in fact it appears normal to others. Sometimes the appearance flaw can be seen by other people if it is pointed out. However, other people view the flaw as being very minor and they would not usually notice it, despite it feeling very obvious to the young person. In this sense, BDD can be described as a problem with lack of confidence.

In BDD, appearance worries are often all-consuming and make the young person feel very distressed. They might feel anxious, depressed, disgusted and/or ashamed of the way they look. Furthermore, a young person with BDD will usually say that their appearance worries get in the way of them doing the things that they want to do. They might avoid specific situations, such as places with bright lights. Or they might avoid a much wider range of situations, like school and social activities. When BDD becomes very severe, young people might struggle to leave their house at all because they are so worried about how they look and what other people will think of them. Young people with BDD also carry out various repetitive behaviours in an attempt to cope with their worries, such as checking or camouflaging (covering up) their perceived flaw/s. These behaviours can be extremely time-consuming and are carried out at the expense of getting on with other important activities, such as seeing friends or doing homework.

If this description sounds familiar to you, the first thing to say is that you are not alone. You might be surprised to hear that BDD is actually relatively common and affects approximately 2% of young people and adults. That means that, on average, in a school with 1000 students, there will be 20 young people with BDD. The disorder affects both boys and girls, and it can start at any age, although it usually begins during teenage years. Unfortunately, BDD often goes undiagnosed because people are too embarrassed to talk about it and there is limited awareness of the disorder. Sometimes people with BDD think that if they tell anyone about their appearance worries, they will seem vain. It is very important to emphasise that BDD is *not* about being vain. In fact, BDD is the opposite of vanity. People with BDD are concerned about perceived flaws in their appearance and typically worry that they look ugly or abnormal.

Do I have BDD or a real flaw in my appearance?

In BDD, young people worry about flaws in their appearance that are generally not noticeable to other people. Sometimes young people with BDD acknowledge this fact and recognise that they are worrying more than they really need to. However, many are convinced that there is actually something physically wrong with their appearance. Even if other people tell them that they look OK, they do not believe it and reassurance does not help. Sometimes young people think that they cannot have BDD because their appearance flaws are real. It is important to try not to get caught up in thinking about whether your appearance concerns are 'real' flaws or not. At the heart of BDD is feeling worried and ashamed about appearance, being distressed and finding it hard to get on with normal life. If this applies to you, then it is possible that you have BDD and it is worthwhile seeking help (see Chapter 6 'Treatment for BDD').

What are common BDD worries?

The majority of people with BDD worry about multiple aspects of their appearance. The most common concerns are facial features such as skin, hair, nose, eyes, chin and teeth. However, any part of the body can become a focus of concern, including genitalia. Some people with BDD do not worry about specific features but instead say that they feel generally ugly. Others say that they do not mind their individual features but feel that they do not 'fit together' properly. Sometimes young people worry that they look too feminine (e.g. their shoulders are too narrow) or masculine (e.g. their hands are too big), or that they do not look right compared with their family or cultural group (e.g. their skin is too light or dark).

What are common
BDD-related behaviours?

Young people with BDD typically carry out a range of repetitive behaviours in an effort to cope with their appearance concerns. For example, they might try to camouflage or conceal their perceived flaw by covering it with clothing (e.g. wearing a hat or hood to cover their hair), applying excessive amounts of make-up (e.g. foundation to cover their skin) or using other parts of their body (e.g. holding their hand in front of their mouth when they speak to cover their teeth). They can also spend huge amounts of time examining their appearance in mirrors and other reflective surfaces (e.g. windows). Conversely, young people might avoid looking in mirrors as they find this too distressing. It is also very common for young people with BDD to spend a lot of time carrying out grooming routines, such as applying make-up and cosmetic products. Again, it is important to reiterate that these behaviours are not driven by vanity, but instead are fuelled by anxiety about appearance. Young people with BDD are not striving for perfection in their appearance, but rather are trying to correct their perceived defects in an attempt to look 'normal'.

Many young people with BDD say that they frequently examine other people's appearance and compare it with their own. Sometimes this is done online, with young people spending huge amounts of time comparing images with their own appearance. It also common to attempt to seek reassurance – for example, by repeatedly asking family members if they look OK. Some young people with BDD engage in harmful behaviours in an attempt to improve their appearance. For example, they might repeatedly pick their skin in an effort to rid themselves of perceived blemishes, which is often counterproductive as it can give rise to scarring and further fuel appearance anxiety.

What is the difference between BDD and an eating disorder?

BDD is not the only condition that is characterised by concerns about appearance. People with eating disorders also worry about the way they look. The main difference between eating disorders and BDD is that eating disorders are characterised by concerns about body weight and shape, which lead to unhealthy patterns of eating (e.g. binging or restricted eating) in an attempt to lose weight. This is different to BDD which does not typically involve general concerns about being too fat or weighing too much, and is not usually associated with eating difficulties.

What is muscle dysmorphia?

Muscle dysmorphia is a particular form of BDD in which young people are concerned about muscle size and shape. It is more common in boys than girls, and often involves worrying about looking too small or weak. As a result, young people with muscle dysmorphia often go to great lengths to 'bulk up' by changing their diet (e.g. following high-protein diets and taking supplements) and spending excessive amounts of time exercising.

How do I know if I have BDD?

BDD should be diagnosed by a qualified healthcare professional and you should not try to self-diagnose. However, you can get a sense of whether or not you are likely to be suffering from BDD by answering the questions in the box below.

DO I HAVE BDD?

1. Do you spend an hour or more every day worrying about your appearance?

2. Do you find yourself carrying out lots of behaviours (e.g. mirror checking, grooming) and/or mental acts (e.g. comparing your appearance with other people's) in an effort to cope with your appearance worries?

3. Do your appearance worries make you feel miserable (e.g. anxious, depressed or ashamed) and/or get in the way of daily activities (e.g. socialising, going to school or leisure activities)?

4. Are your appearance concerns focused on being too fat or weighing too much?

If you answer 'yes' to questions 1–3 and 'no' to question 4, it is possible that you are experiencing BDD and you should speak to a healthcare professional.

If you think you might have BDD, it is important to seek help. In the first instance, you can speak to your general practitioner (GP). He or she will probably refer you for an assessment with a mental health professional who will help you to figure out whether or not you are suffering from BDD. This process might sound daunting, but seeking help is the first step towards recovery. If you do have BDD, seeking help is very important because effective treatment is available (see Chapter 6 'Treatment for BDD').

THINGS TO REMEMBER

✓ BDD is characterised by appearance worries which cause distress and get in the way of day-to-day life.

✓ BDD is relatively common and usually starts during adolescence.

✓ Young people with BDD are not vain.

✓ Try not to get caught up in analysing whether your appearance concerns are 'real' physical flaws or not. Instead, focus on whether or not your concerns are making you miserable and getting in the way of everyday life.

✓ If you think you might have BDD, it is important to seek help.

2

WHY DO PEOPLE GET BDD?

This chapter will:

- help you to understand more about possible causes of BDD

- outline the biological, environmental and psychological factors that increase the likelihood of developing BDD.

So, if you have been diagnosed with BDD, you might be asking yourself, 'Why do I have BDD and what caused it?' Similarly, it is often common for families and relatives to express a desire to know what 'caused' the illness.

Unfortunately, we still don't know exactly what causes BDD, but scientists are working on this. We do know that it is no one's fault if you have BDD (not yours, your parents' or anybody else's) and no one is to blame for it. We also know that – as with many other mental health conditions – BDD is probably not caused by one specific thing, but it is more likely the result of a combination of things that make people more vulnerable to developing the condition during their lifetime. Although scientists are still working on finding out what causes BDD, the 'risk' or 'vulnerability' factors for BDD can be grouped into three categories: biological, sociocultural (or 'environmental') and psychological.

Biological 'risk' factors

When we think of the biological 'risk' factors that make someone more sensitive to getting BDD, we think of genes, brain chemicals and areas of the brain. It has been found that BDD runs in families; in fact, up to 10% of BDD sufferers have another family member with the same condition. Scientists think this is partly because individuals inherit the 'BDD genes'. Unfortunately, we still have not identified the 'BDD genes' and it is unlikely that there will be a single gene causing BDD; this means research is still under way to find out how genes may be involved in BDD. Although the risk of having BDD is increased if you have biological relatives with BDD or other anxiety and mood problems, it is important also to know that not everyone who has a genetic vulnerability to BDD will develop the condition.

In terms of other biological factors, scientists think that the reduced activity of a brain chemical called serotonin may account for the symptoms of BDD. A type of medication called selective serotonin reuptake inhibitors (SSRIs for short) has been found to improve BDD symptoms; this medication blocks the reabsorption of serotonin in the brain (making more serotonin available), which helps to reduce symptoms (see Chapter 6 'Treatment for BDD').

Finally, a number of brain areas – such as the amygdala, striatum and other brain regions – may be involved in explaining why certain people develop BDD. In particular, it has been found that people with BDD have reduced activity in brain areas involved with processing general visual information (what we see). This reduced brain activity may explain why people with BDD zoom in or over-focus on details of their appearance at the expense of the bigger picture.

Sociocultural 'risk' factors

Sociocultural or 'environmental' factors can increase the chance of developing BDD. For example, negative or upsetting experiences in childhood (e.g. being teased, bullied or rejected by peers) can contribute to someone feeling more self-conscious about how they look and developing body image concerns. Young people with BDD often tell us that their body image concerns began around the same time they were being teased or bullied in school. This doesn't mean that everyone who is teased or bullied goes on to develop BDD, but these negative experiences can increase or shape a person's anxiety about appearance and/or how they ought to look.

Sometimes people experience events that are frightening or stressful (e.g. an accident, moving home, the death of a loved one, loss of a friendship, family stress). These difficult life situations can sometimes bring on BDD symptoms. We know that BDD symptoms can worsen during stressful times, suggesting that stress plays a role in BDD.

Social and cultural pressures to be 'beautiful' and 'flawless' are important (unspecific) risk factors for BDD as they contribute to body image fixation and anxiety about appearance. We are surrounded by ads, videos and images selling the idea of the 'perfect look', which we ought to achieve by buying a certain cosmetic product, dietary supplement, outfit, exercise machine, etc. These standards of beauty are unrealistic and may make us feel more sensitive or self-conscious about how we look or trigger our need to improve our appearance. The pressure to achieve physical perfection can be a contributing factor for those with a vulnerability to body image concerns or BDD, but this does not cause BDD.

Psychological 'risk' factors

Other factors that are known to increase the risk of developing or triggering BDD are called psychological 'risk' factors. As mentioned earlier, scientists think there are differences in the way people with BDD process visual information (what they see). It has been found that BDD sufferers are less effective at 'global visual processing', so are more likely to over-focus on details when looking at images of faces or objects, at the expense of the 'bigger' picture. It is thought that too much focus on details may contribute to (and maintain) BDD.

Certain personality traits – for example, perfectionism – and anxious and/or inhibited personality styles are also considered (unspecific) risk or vulnerability factors for

BDD. Individuals with BDD have been found to report higher levels of perfectionism than people without BDD. Individuals with personalities that value being 'perfect' may try to reach unrealistically high standards and experience a sense of failure and self-criticism if they are unable to achieve those goals. Someone with this personality may be more likely to develop BDD; for example, they may notice even minor flaws in appearance and struggle to accept or tolerate imperfections, contributing to the development of body image concerns.

Experts in the field of BDD often refer to 'aesthetic sensitivity' as a specific psychological risk factor for the development of BDD. This is the idea that individuals vary in their 'aesthetical skills' (or view of beauty); in a similar way, individuals may vary in their 'musicality' (view of music). These experts believe that people with BDD may have a higher developed sense of aestheticality and therefore may be more self-conscious and aware of variations in appearance. In support of this idea is the finding that many more people with this condition end up having an education or occupation in arts and design compared with people without BDD. As illustrated below and throughout this book, many of the young people we see in our clinic do indeed share an artistic talent. Research findings also suggest that individuals who place a higher value or importance on beauty may be more vulnerable to developing BDD.

Robert Burton

Robert Burton

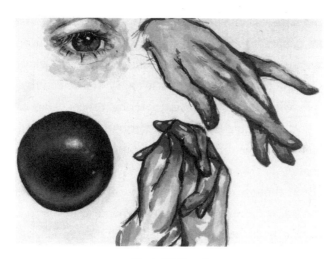

Katie Holland

Elias Marchetti

Another important vulnerability factor for BDD (and anxiety more generally) is the bias for threatening information. A recent study found that BDD sufferers are more likely to misinterpret facial expressions as angry and rejecting than people without BDD. Misinterpreting others' glances as angry and rejecting is likely to contribute, maintain and/or reinforce the person's concerns about perceived flaws and ugliness.

Even though we cannot be sure of what causes BDD, we do know there are effective treatments available to help overcome body image concerns and BDD (see Chapter 6 'Treatment for BDD' to find out more).

THINGS TO REMEMBER

✓ It is no one's fault if you have BDD.

✓ We don't know the causes of BDD yet, but a number of biological, sociocultural/ environmental and psychological 'risk' factors are known to increase the likelihood of someone developing BDD.

✓ Biological 'risk' factors include:

   ○ having biological relative(s) with BDD or another mental health condition such as anxiety and depression

- an imbalance of a brain chemical called serotonin

- differences in levels of activity in certain brain areas.

✓ Environmental 'risk' factors include:

- negative childhood experiences (e.g. teasing/bullying)

- stress

- societal pressure or expectations of beauty.

✓ Psychological 'risk' factors include:

- a tendency to over-focus on details

- showing a greater degree of 'aesthetic sensitivity' (or aesthetic skills) and placing a higher value on appearance

- exhibiting certain personality traits (e.g. perfectionism)

- misinterpreting facial expressions as angry and rejecting.

3

THE IMPACT OF BDD

This chapter will tell you the ways in which BDD can affect:

- mood and how people feel

- social life, relationships and hobbies

- how family members feel and behave

- learning and time spent at school or work

- how much money people spend.

Before we discuss the impact of BDD, it is important to stress that there are effective treatments available (see Chapter 6 'Treatment for BDD'). We highlight this now as it is important to know that what we discuss in this chapter can get better.

Mood

If you are experiencing BDD, you will probably have noticed a number of changes to your mood. Individuals with BDD have described lots of negative emotions, including anxiety, sadness or low mood, poor self-esteem (thinking that they are useless or worthless) or feeling disgusted about themselves. They may find it hard to enjoy things that they liked doing before, have less energy, have difficulty concentrating or have problems with eating or sleeping (either too much or too little). As appearance has become such a major focus in the life of a person with BDD, all of the other things that may have been important before and given them a sense of achievement become smaller and often a cause of more anxiety. Sadly, BDD and feelings about it can often be kept hidden, which means that a person is left to manage these difficult things alone.

Like many others with BDD, you may have tried to seek help but felt misunderstood about these difficulties. You may have received a different diagnosis (such as depression, social anxiety or an eating disorder) or you may have had your concerns dismissed as 'normal' teenage worries. If you have been offered a less helpful type of treatment as a result of this, it is possible that you have been left feeling even more misunderstood and hopeless about the possibility of getting better. You may have turned to using drugs or alcohol in an attempt to manage your feelings. At its most severe, it is not uncommon for people with BDD to feel as though they do not want to be alive as a result of their appearance worries and feelings.

Social impact

You will probably have found that BDD has made it more difficult to be around others, perhaps because you want to hide your physical appearance from them. Sometimes young people tell us it is hard to make eye contact, speak or interact with others. This could be because you do not want to do or say anything that may draw others' attention to your appearance. When in social situations, you may direct most of your focus and attention towards your own appearance, and so you do not get to enjoy other people's company properly or find out about their views.

Some young people give up going to clubs or teams that they have previously enjoyed or others may feel that they need to spend lots of time at the gym or exercising (but this tends to take place alone and leave little time for other social activities). Being with friends or other people can lead to comparing physical features with them, which can cause distress and get in the way of friendships. You may also be worried that other people will think that you are vain if they notice how much time you are spending trying to check or improve your appearance. Sex or relationships with boyfriends and girlfriends can be avoided due to a person's difficulty with their appearance or because BDD behaviours take up so much time that it is impossible to spend enough time together. At its worst, BDD may stop people from leaving their home or bedroom entirely.

Family life and relationships

Members of your family may have noticed themselves behaving in a particular way to try to reduce your anxiety. This could include helping you with grooming or checking routines or giving you lots of reassurance about your appearance. Although their efforts may have given you some relief at first, any benefits tend to reduce over time until they become unhelpful. For example, young people have reported that when relatives try to reassure them with phrases such as 'You look fine', this can make them feel misunderstood or that they are being lied to.

Often individuals experiencing BDD may not agree at first that this diagnosis applies to them. They may think it is a physical problem and not a psychological one. When disagreement arises within families about the true nature of the 'problem', tensions can run high. A young person may be very frustrated by a parent who doesn't see things the same way as them and vice versa. We have been told by families that this can lead to physical aggression, particularly if a young person believes that their parent is preventing a compulsion or blocking their access to cosmetic procedures or surgery. Unfortunately, we have also heard of parents or siblings commenting negatively about a young person's appearance during arguments or withholding access to compulsions as a 'punishment'. When BDD leads to dangerous or extreme behaviours, such as self-harm, not eating or becoming housebound, family members can becoming overwhelmingly worried and feel helpless to make things better for their loved one. There can often be lots of guilt, resentment or frustration experienced on both sides.

It is easy to see how family conflict can develop as a result of BDD and cause additional distress in the home. We know BDD and other anxiety difficulties can run in families. When this is the case, families may find it even harder to work out how to respond to one another's appearance concerns or feel that they have less energy or emotional strength to manage a family member's difficulties in addition to their own.

Impact on school

You may be one of the many young people who find that BDD impacts upon their education. As some young people with BDD find it hard to leave their home at all, attending school can seem impossible. The long routines carried out before leaving the house (e.g. spending hours on hair and make-up, trying on multiple outfits and checking appearance) lead to frequent lateness. Young people have told us that they have got into trouble at school for this or for other reasons relating to BDD, such as wearing make-up or clothing that are against school rules.

The overwhelming effort of managing BDD means that you might feel exhausted at school and lack the energy needed to participate. Some of the BDD behaviours arising at school include leaving lessons to check appearance or reapply make-up in bathroom mirrors. Lots of young people report avoiding PE or dance lessons in particular because these trigger greater BDD thoughts. Appearance may remain on your mind in class, as you spend time worrying about how you look. This often leads to being unable to follow instructions or avoiding taking part in class activities for fear of drawing more attention to your appearance. Some young people have told us that they get stuck checking and comparing pictures online when they are given access to computers in lessons, or feel compelled to look at photos or social media accounts on their phone. When these difficulties reduce an individual's ability to pay attention to their school work, their grades may begin to drop.

Financial impact

It is known that some people with appearance worries can become so dissatisfied and distressed about their appearance that they see surgery or other cosmetic procedures as the only option. These can cost a lot of money and many young people do not have a regular income of their own. Younger people may be less able than adults to access major procedures in a clinic; nevertheless, the cost of frequent salon treatments can quickly add up. For example, a person may be paying for waxing, tanning, eyebrow shaping or eyelash extensions far more than their friends without BDD, as well as other beauty products or clothing. Other young people may be spending money on muscle-building products (including steroids). With public transport leading to distress, in many cases there may be other additional expenses such as taxi fares or petrol costs. As with school, maintaining a job can be very difficult for a young person with BDD, so they may not be able to rely on the money that this would provide. We also hear from parents who have themselves given up work to care for their child with BDD. The urge to carry out BDD compulsions can lead young people to do things that they would not otherwise consider, even things that are dangerous and illegal. This includes stealing products from shops or taking money from parents or relatives without permission.

THINGS TO REMEMBER

✓ BDD can cause problems in a wide range of areas, all of which can have a catastrophic effect on the quality of life that young people experience.

✓ BDD can also cause problems for family and friends.

✓ Some of the impact of BDD can be seen by others, but some can remain hidden and this can delay or prevent young people from accessing the right kind of support for BDD.

4

COSMETIC TREATMENTS

This chapter will tell you:

- what cosmetic treatments are and whether they work when you have BDD

- the risks involved with using cosmetic treatments if you have BDD.

What are cosmetic treatments?

Cosmetic treatments cover an entire range of procedures. Cosmetic treatments can involve serious operations and surgeries such as rhinoplasties ('nose jobs') or breast augmentations ('boob jobs'). There are also a vast number of less costly, and quicker, procedures which are performed in beauty or dermatology clinics. These include things like having botox, getting lip fillers or having moles removed for non-medical reasons. Below are some more examples of what we mean when we talk about cosmetic treatments.

TYPES OF COSMETIC TREATMENTS

- rhinoplasty ('nose job')

- botox

- surgery of various types

- laser treatments (e.g. to reduce wrinkles in the skin or skin irregularities)

- dermatological procedures (e.g. chemical peels)

- dentistry work

- electrolysis (e.g. for hair removal)

- collagen injections or fillers (e.g. to treat laughter lines or wrinkles or to make lips/cheeks appear fuller)

- breast augmentation/implants ('boob job')

- labiaplasty (surgery to change the appearance of genitalia).

If you have considered getting any of these done, have spent time researching on the internet to find a practitioner to perform these procedures or are saving up money to take your plans forward, you are not alone. We know from both seeing young people in our clinic and from research that around 40% of young people with BDD either desire or have taken steps towards having cosmetic treatments.

Why does cosmetic treatment seem like the right treatment?

As explained in earlier chapters, BDD affects your perception of yourself. You view your appearance in a way that is different to those around you and conclude the problem is on the outside rather than being about how you feel about yourself and your appearance – what we call your *body image*. It makes sense therefore that you try to 'correct' things on the outside in order to feel better on the inside. The problem with this is that research and clinical experience suggest that no matter how much you try to 'fix' your appearance outwardly, this won't improve your body image and how you feel about your appearance if you have BDD.

The downsides to cosmetic treatment when you have BDD

A few studies have asked young people with BDD how they felt following cosmetic treatments and found that most often young people said that they were dissatisfied with their cosmetic treatment and that their body part still looked 'ugly' or 'not right'. Other people may say they are satisfied with the body part which has been treated but then go on to develop concerns about other aspects of their appearance. In the most upsetting cases, people have reported being *more* unhappy about their appearance following cosmetic treatments and feeling hopeless and suicidal as a result. Cosmetic treatments also cost a lot of money. Young people have told us they have stolen money, used their parents' credit cards or even signed up to escort agencies in efforts to get money together for surgery. Young people have told us they have lied about their age in an attempt to get surgery without their parents' consent, or, have tried to find surgeons on the internet who are prepared to perform treatments without carrying out the necessary assessments and checks.

'I still want to go ahead with a cosmetic treatment'

Even after learning how unlikely it is that cosmetic treatments will help, some young people with BDD still want to pursue this option. Any doctor carrying out cosmetic surgery must adhere to codes of conduct and care as outlined by the General Medical Council, the British Association of Aesthetic Plastic Surgeons and the Royal College of Surgeons. Young people should be supported appropriately if they decide to go ahead with plans for cosmetic treatments, especially surgery. Families and young people have told us it is most useful to have an open and honest conversation about their plans for cosmetic treatments and their appearance concerns with their families and the professionals carrying out the cosmetic treatments. In some cases, it might also be a good idea to discuss your plans with a mental health professional, especially if you have a diagnosis of BDD already. Although there are risks involved in pursuing cosmetic treatments when you have BDD, it is better to have people around you and a support plan in place, rather than doing something in secret and using services that might not follow the necessary procedures. The professionals carrying out cosmetic treatments should know about your appearance concerns and BDD diagnosis if you have one, to ensure they can support you through this process in the safest possible way.

In this book we will talk about how getting treatment to focus on what is going on inside (i.e. your body image and thoughts and feelings) and working on building your confidence and self-worth can change the way you view your appearance. Many young people find at the end of having psychological treatment for BDD that they no longer want to change parts of themselves using cosmetic treatments.

THINGS TO REMEMBER

✓ Desiring cosmetic treatments is common in young people with BDD.

✓ It is highly unlikely that having cosmetic treatments will be the solution to your distress and worry about your appearance. There is a chance it could actually make things worse.

✓ Many young people with BDD no longer want to have cosmetic treatments after they have had psychological therapy specifically for BDD. Try this first.

✓ If you are sure that, despite the research, you want to go ahead with cosmetic treatments, it is best to do this in an open and transparent way with your family and the professionals carrying out the cosmetic treatment. Tell them about your appearance concerns so they can keep you safe.

5

THE INTERNET AND SOCIAL MEDIA

This chapter will tell you:

- why so many young people with BDD spend hours on the internet trying to find solutions to their difficulties

- the risks involved with using the internet and social media if you have BDD

- tips on how to manage the problems and risks of the internet and social media when you have BDD.

Let's start this section by saying up front that we are not going to recommend that you stop using the internet, social media or your apps! We know that the internet and social media play an important role in young people's lives and that there are lots of benefits and fun to be had with technology. However, what we do want to focus on in this section is when our relationship with social media becomes problematic. This is when you feel anxious, distressed, ashamed or depressed using your devices, instead of feeling happy or excited.

Apart from researching cosmetic treatments (as discussed in Chapter 4 'Cosmetic treatments'), you might be spending hours comparing yourself with others, uploading pictures of yourself, visiting blogs or watching make-up tutorials, all in an attempt to find the solution to your concerns about appearance. You might also use social media to try to get reassurance about your appearance by signing up to sites where appearance is rated. The risk is that you can quickly get into a vicious cycle of being overly focused on your appearance. You may also become exposed to unhealthy messages about appearance, which can in turn affect your body image. When you excessively use websites that focus on trying to 'correct' or 'better' appearance, you can give appearance more importance than it needs. Many websites are designed for adults or those over 18; you cannot be sure who you are talking to and not all sites are properly regulated. You might be asked to send intimate pictures of yourself or you might feel compelled to meet strangers you have met on the internet. You should not send any photos of yourself unless you would be happy about other people seeing these. Once you send them, you have no control over how these photos are used.

Cyber-bullying

Bullying is a problem that affects many teens and nowadays bullying can occur 24/7 via 'cyber-bullying'. The problem is, if you have BDD already, it is likely that cyber-bullying is going to have an even bigger impact on your mood and self-worth because you already dislike yourself in some ways. Most cyber-bullies or 'trolls' try to break up friendship groups or verbally abuse people and tend to pick on the things people already feel vulnerable or insecure about. Many young people with BDD have told us that cyber-bullies will make abusive comments about their appearance. If you have been using apps and social media to try to get reassurance about your appearance, or others can see that appearance is very important to you because of the sites you visit or things you upload, cyber-bullies might use this information. In fact, cyber-bullies can go as far as actively encouraging you to hurt yourself or commit suicide. Remember, social media is poorly controlled; anyone can make an app, and some people who post on blogs do so to promote unhelpful messages that are driven by their own agendas. It is important to tell someone if you are being cyber-bullied, and many websites have functions where you can block or manage bullies/trolls.

Is what we see on the internet realistic?

We are all now able to use advancing technology to create unrealistic and unattainable images of ourselves and others. The problem is that you then compare yourself against such pictures, forgetting that these are not what real people look like; they are highly selected images which have often been put through many filters and altered. Remember, not even models look like their pictures!

TOP TIPS FOR MANAGING YOUR RELATIONSHIP WITH SOCIAL MEDIA AND APPS

- Set limits for how many times a day you will access the app/website.

- Set a limit for how long you will spend on a certain website/app each time you use it.

- Set small targets limiting your time using apps/websites and then go longer between checks and reward yourself when you are successful.

- Choose another fun or distracting app during the time you would normally check your unhelpful apps.

- Find positive, funny or inspirational people to follow instead.

- Avoid or delete unhelpful apps/websites.

- Always be cautious about uploading any pictures of yourself and never send nude pictures to others.

THINGS TO REMEMBER

✓ You can change your relationship with social media, the internet and apps so that the internet remains something which is fun and enjoyable.

✓ Cyber-bullying is common and there are many things you can do to prevent it; tell an adult and check out the helpful websites in the back of this book.

✓ Remember that social media and the internet are poorly regulated; you don't know who is creating which app/website for what purpose.

✓ Spending an excessive amount of time on apps and social media centred on appearance can actually make your worries worse and affect your body image.

✓ Pictures in the media are highly selected and often altered using a lot of technology and filters.

Rory Daniels

6

TREATMENT FOR BDD

This chapter will tell you:

- which treatments are available for BDD

- what psychological treatment looks like

- which medication options can be considered

- things that can get in the way of accessing the right treatment

- how to get treatment for BDD.

Treatments for BDD

If you feel that you are suffering from BDD, or you have been diagnosed with BDD, the good news is that treatments are available. Treatments for BDD have only been developed fairly recently, but the research that has been carried out shows some promising results. The best evidence so far supports two possible treatment options, which can be delivered independently of each other or can be given together. One treatment is psychological, specifically cognitive behaviour therapy (CBT). The other option is medication, and this includes a number of different alternatives.

Cognitive behaviour therapy for BDD

Psychological therapy is often referred to as 'talking therapy', but it involves more than just talking. Psychological therapy is when you meet with a therapist to work on how you are feeling and the experiences and worries you are having. There are many different types of psychological therapy available but not all of them work for all difficulties. Anybody seeking psychological help for BDD should be offered cognitive behaviour therapy (CBT) as this is the only psychological treatment which has been proven to work for BDD. In the UK, CBT is the treatment recommended by the National Institute for Health and Care Excellence (NICE), which provides treatment guidelines based on the best available evidence. It is only fairly recently that clinicians and researchers have been developing psychological treatments for BDD, so treatments are still evolving and they may look different in the future. Based on the research so far, we know that there are a few components that should be included in a good course of CBT for BDD for it to be as effective as possible.

A good-quality course of CBT for BDD should include meeting with your therapist weekly for sessions of about 60 minutes each. You might need around 20 sessions in total, but this can vary quite a bit. Your therapist should discuss with you how your family is likely to be involved in your treatment. It can be really important for your family to be a part of your sessions, but their degree of involvement in your treatment will depend on how much they have to do for your BDD, as well as other factors such as your age. See the box below for what CBT for BDD should ideally cover.

KEY COMPONENTS OF CBT FOR BDD

- Learning about BDD, anxiety and key psychological processes associated with this condition.

- Understanding your own BDD – in particular, the behaviours that you engage in and how these fuel worries about appearance and difficult emotions.

- Practising reducing your BDD-related behaviours, with the help of your therapist and maybe also your family and friends. This will involve actively carrying out tasks and challenges in sessions. It is important to note that this process is done gradually, in steps that feel manageable for you.

- It is really important that you also carry out these tasks in between sessions (this is often called 'therapy homework'), in order to build your confidence.

Depending on your specific difficulties with BDD, your therapist might consider adding other components from the box below.

ADDITIONAL CBT FOR BDD COMPONENTS

- Practising how to shift your focus of attention from your appearance to the world around you.

- Learning how to use mirrors in a helpful and non-judgemental way.

- Working directly with specific unhelpful thoughts you might be having.

- Working through relevant, difficult experiences from your past such as appearance-related bullying.

- Help with improving your self-esteem.

THINGS TO REMEMBER

✓ The only psychological treatment that has been proven to work for BDD is CBT.

✓ Your therapist may use a range of techniques, but there are some key things that any course of CBT should include, such as active tasks to resist BDD behaviours.

✓ CBT sessions should be frequent and you should have clear tasks to complete at home after every session ('therapy homework').

Medication for BDD

In addition to psychological therapy for BDD, there is good evidence that medication can be helpful. Typically, young people should try a psychological therapy first, but this is not always easily available. Medication can be considered as an option on its own. More usually, however, people would choose to use medication for BDD alongside CBT.

Medication treatment for BDD should be started and carefully monitored by a mental health specialist. Most typically, this would be a psychiatrist or a prescribing nurse in a mental health team.

There are several medications that can be helpful in tackling BDD. The same medications can also help if you are having other sorts of difficulties, including low mood (depression) or other forms of anxiety. When considering medication, it is important that you discuss these things with the specialist helping you.

The most common type of medications used for BDD belong to a group of treatments called selective serotonin reuptake inhibitors, or SSRIs for short. They have been around for several decades now. Despite understandable worries about starting a medication like this, for most young people they are typically helpful, effective and safe, and can be used without any worrying side effects. There are many SSRI medications and young people would try one of them at a time. SSRIs often used for BDD include sertraline (Lustral), fluoxetine (Prozac), fluvoxamine (Faverin), paroxetine (Seroxat) and escitalopram (Cipralex), among others.

If you think you want to start a medication like this, it is important to get the facts straight and have a detailed conversation about the medication before deciding. Most young people ask someone close to them, such as their parents, to help them think about this and come to a decision.

It is not uncommon for young people with BDD to have other issues, outside of their emotional difficulties, to consider as well. Sometimes these issues include other common things such as tics, attention deficit hyperactivity disorder or autism spectrum disorder. Physical health difficulties also need to be carefully considered in making a treatment plan. The result could mean choosing different medication, additional medications or planning additional tests and assessments before starting treatment.

There are some important things to think about when trying medication to help improve BDD worries. First, we know the medications should be increased slowly and carefully over the course of a few weeks. This allows any possible side effects to be carefully managed or avoided, by allowing your body to get used to the treatment gradually. The medications used to help with BDD need to be increased to a high dose, higher than for other kinds of difficulties such as depression, which is another good reason to increase slowly. The next important thing to remember is that it can take a long time for the medication to start to work. A trial of medication should be about three months of an adequate dose, so it is important to be patient and not expect overnight results. Because of this, the professional prescribing any medication for BDD should take careful note of your symptoms, so that you and they can be clear when things are starting to improve. When a young person and the professionals involved in their care feel a medication is really not working after giving it a good try, they often opt to try another SSRI instead.

Part of understanding any medication that you might consider starting is to learn about possible side effects. About 40% of people taking an SSRI medication will experience a side effect of one type or another. The majority of these side effects happen in the first two to three weeks of taking the medication. Headaches and tummy upsets are among the most common issues. These are usually mild, easily managed and, with good support, will typically go away quite quickly and without causing any worrying problems. It is really important to know how to get hold of the correct specialist advice. Our experience is that if medication treatment is carefully planned and managed, the majority of young people with BDD are able to take this medication without any worrying problems. They also typically find that medication is a helpful way to tackle BDD.

Young people often ask when they should stop their medication. Most commonly, people with BDD are asked to stay on their medication for at least six months after they are feeling better. This can seem like a long time, but stopping too early can often mean the difficulties come back again. It is important when you are thinking about stopping medication that you do so in a planned way. This plan would include the people who support you, including the specialists and others such as your family.

THINGS TO REMEMBER

✓ Medication is an effective treatment for BDD but is best used alongside CBT.

✓ Medication should be carefully explained to you by a specialist who is experienced in using these sorts of treatments with young people.

✓ The positive effects of medication for BDD can be slow to build up, so it is important to be patient.

✓ Side effects can occur but they typically settle and disappear.

✓ You should keep taking the medication for at least six months after you are feeling better.

✓ You should always know how to get hold of the advice and support you need if you are taking medication for BDD.

Barriers to accessing treatment

Even though treatments for BDD are available, many young people and their families say that accessing that treatment is not always a straightforward process. There are a few different reasons for this. They might feel embarrassed and ashamed, or they might feel that it's a physical problem, so no one can really help. Not only can this leave the young person feeling isolated and alone, but it also means they are unlikely to take the steps needed to see a professional who may be able to help. However, BDD is unlikely to just get better by itself, so if you do think that this sounds like something you are going through, it is really important that you try to reach out to someone. Try to think of one person who you feel might understand even just a little of how you are feeling. You might even want to give them this book as a way of explaining what you are going through and to give them some guidance on how they might be able to help you.

Another factor that sometimes gets in the way of people getting the help they need is that BDD is still not really well understood by everyone. Although professionals might have heard or read about BDD, they might not necessarily be experienced in recognising it. Lots of practitioners say they find it particularly difficult to distinguish BDD from other disorders which seem similar, such as social anxiety or depression. The good news is that this situation is slowly changing, although there is still some way to go before BDD is as recognisable as other disorders. If you do feel that you may be experiencing symptoms of BDD, but that the professionals trying to help you might not be getting your diagnosis quite right, this book could be a good resource to help bridge that gap.

As we mentioned earlier in this chapter, medication can help with the symptoms of BDD for many people. However, you may hear a lot of things that worry you about medications, from friends, family or from the internet. It is therefore really important that you ask questions and get the right answers if those worries are getting in the way of treatment. We know that if these worries are talked about openly, then people may get the quality of information they need to make informed decisions. Specialists should always give you honest, open and clear information, in order to help you make clear decisions about your treatment package.

How to access treatment for BDD

If you are keen to access treatment for BDD, you should speak to your primary care physician – in the UK this is your general practitioner (GP) – who can talk to you about how to get mental health treatment in your local area. This usually involves a referral to a team of psychologists, psychiatrists and other healthcare practitioners, who offer support to young people with a range of mental health difficulties. They can offer you an assessment of your difficulties and talk about treatment options with you. Further advice and support is available from a number of charitable organisations, details of which can be found at the back of this book.

THINGS TO REMEMBER

✓ BDD is very unlikely to get better without the right treatment, so it is important that you try to get the help you need.

✓ Practitioners are still learning about BDD, so you might need to work a little harder to have your difficulties properly recognised than you would if you were suffering from a more widely understood condition.

✓ This book could be a good resource to start those conversations with people and open the door to accessing the help you need.

✓ Poor-quality information about medications can sometimes get in the way of young people using this effective treatment for BDD.

✓ If you want to access treatment for BDD, speak to your primary care physician (e.g. your GP).

7

WHAT CAN FAMILIES, FRIENDS AND CARERS DO TO HELP?

This chapter will tell you:

- how to recognise there is a problem

- how to get help

- how families can manage things from day to day

- what family members can do to support CBT.

Recognising there is a problem

It is often difficult with teenagers to know if concerns about appearance are a 'normal' part of being an adolescent or whether it is BDD. The biggest giveaway is if the preoccupation with their appearance and associated behaviours cause significant distress and interfere with their life; for example, they may be late to school and events or avoid them altogether because of appearance concerns and/ or because of the extensive rituals they need to carry out before leaving the home. There may be other signs which are covered in Chapter 1 'What is BDD and do I have it?' and Chapter 3 'The impact of BDD'.

If you suspect your child has BDD, it is important to share this with them in a calm and non-judgemental way. It is helpful to avoid getting into a discussion about the content of their appearance concerns and instead focus on the distress and interference this is causing. It is important you share with them that you know they are not being vain and that you understand they are suffering because of their worries. You may wish to share this book with them to see if they can relate to what has been described.

Your child may be relieved that this has been recognised as a problem, even though they may not see it as BDD. It is important to keep emphasising the distress and interference aspects of the disorder and reassuring them that there is help available to manage their distress. You can give them information on treatment and support to help them understand what is on offer (see Chapter 6 'Treatment for BDD'). If your child demonstrates any risk issues such as suicidal thoughts or self-harm, it is important you seek mental health support immediately.

Getting help

If your child is unsure about seeking support, you can approach your primary care physician (e.g. your GP) or a mental health service to raise your concerns. You can share with the practitioner that you suspect your child has BDD and discuss with them a way forward to support your child to get treatment. Ideally, your child should join you to seek support, but if they refuse to, do not let that stop you from sharing your concerns with a professional. Your child should be offered a mental health assessment, following which treatment options should be explored. It is vital that the assessment explores BDD as a possible diagnosis, as often clinicians can mistake symptoms as depression, social anxiety or an eating disorder. It may be helpful to take this book and other information with you to ensure BDD is assessed.

Managing from day to day

We know that BDD can take over family life and day-to-day routines can be compromised and disrupted because of the disorder. Giving reassurance and facilitating avoidance and/or behaviours in relation to appearance concerns are common ways families can be drawn into their child's BDD. Although this can help reduce the young person's distress in the short term, we also know it reinforces the problem in the long term – before you know it, BDD has taken over all of your lives. It is often very difficult when your child is seeking reassurance or if they pull you into conversations about their appearance. Although it may be hard, try not to get into conversations about appearance concerns, and don't argue or try to convince them they don't look bad. This can often be a source of arguments and tension, so the less you discuss it, the better. Rather than discussing what they perceive to be wrong with their appearance or trying to talk them out of their BDD beliefs, it may be more helpful to acknowledge their distress instead.

Your child may not only seek reassurance but may also want products and procedures to improve their appearance. It is important to explore with your child, in calmer moments, what is reasonable to expect from you and gently support them to consider how these behaviours could be reinforcing their appearance worries. They may find it helpful to read Chapter 4 'Cosmetic treatments' and Chapter 5 'The internet and social media' in this book. It is important to come to an agreed plan to manage these requests and to ensure there is consistency across family members. If your child is having CBT, this can be discussed in sessions. It is important to do things step by step and not expect your child to be able to resist all behaviours straight away.

Aggression and angry outbursts are common in people with BDD. It is helpful to notice what triggers these and what happens. In a calm moment, you can discuss with your child what you have noticed and how you can manage this together. As a family, it is important to establish boundaries of what is and is not acceptable in your household. Even if the behaviour is driven by BDD, it is important to keep these boundaries in place. It is hard when you are managing day-to-day life in general as well as supporting your child who has BDD. It is tricky, when they are getting angry and upset, for you not to do the same. However, this is where things can escalate and conflict can arise. If you recognise that this is happening, it is important to try to step away from the situation, to allow things to calm down and then revisit the discussion. It is hard for everyone involved, but remember your child is not doing this on purpose; this is coming from a place of distress.

It is important that you recognise the impact BDD is having on you and that you make sure you have support in place. This may include you having support from a therapist or having someone to speak to in or outside of your family. There are support groups available for parents of BDD sufferers (see 'Recommended reading, resources and organisations'). You must make time for *you* and look after yourself to be in the best place to support your child.

Supporting your child through CBT

If your child is offered CBT, there are things you can do to help them through the process. If possible, it will be helpful to attend the first couple of sessions that cover psychoeducation on BDD to gain a good understanding of the condition and how it works, as well as the techniques to overcome it. Try to join at the end of every session so that you can be given an overview of what was covered in the session and know what homework tasks have been set for the week. Alongside understanding and learning about BDD, parents are often involved in the treatment by helping out as coaches or co-therapists, which may include helping to carry out homework tasks and providing support and encouragement during treatment. Finally, we know that often families are drawn into BDD in various ways (e.g. giving reassurance, providing items for appearance-related rituals, facilitating avoidance). These behaviours maintain the BDD worries and focus on appearance, and therefore become important targets during treatment, so it is helpful for families to receive guidance on what to do. Young people vary in terms of the amount of support they require from their parents when doing homework tasks or how much they want parents involved in treatment. Discuss with your child (and their therapist) how they would like you to support them as they may have some great ideas. With your child and their therapist, plan how to reduce reassurance and involvement with BDD; it is usually more effective to withdraw this support gradually. Progress can seem slow, particularly in the early stages of treatment, and there are likely to be setbacks along the way, so it is important everyone is patient with the process.

MESSAGE FROM A PARENT

Understanding the condition and how it affects your child is vitally important. They will feel supported and better equipped to deal with their BDD and find the strength to work on their recovery.

Recovery can take time and will be challenging for your child and your family. Be patient and continually encourage and motivate them to work on their treatment. You have to be prepared to take on a therapist role, so fully understanding the treatment process is vital!

Be careful with 'safety behaviours' (our son avoided going out, people, showering, wearing ordinary clothes). It is easy to be drawn into these behaviours and become part of the problem by unintentionally fuelling the BDD. It is important to identify whether you are unknowingly exacerbating the problem. Our son spent hours obsessing about his body – he wanted us to agree with how he saw himself. We would respond with positive comments about his appearance, believing we were helping him. We thought it would counteract his negative beliefs, but it was actually feeding his obsession.

If your child asks for your reassurance about their appearance, don't engage. We explained to our son how engaging in these conversations would make his BDD worse and that we would no longer respond. Eventually, he stopped talking to us about it, which made him a lot calmer and not so obsessed.

BDD children can get angry – especially when we're encouraging them to do things they're avoiding or to limit ritual behaviours. We now know when to back off. Motivate and encourage them, but if they're too anxious, constantly pushing won't achieve anything. Back off and try another time. Don't give up! They need you to encourage them to get better.

Look after you! Try to stay positive (at times this seems impossible), but you must continue to have hope.

Emma Beardsworth

THINGS TO REMEMBER

✓ BDD can have a significant impact on family life and lead carers to be drawn into the BDD concerns and appearance-related behaviours.

✓ Understand that your child is not behaving this way on purpose; they are distressed, but there is support out there for them.

✓ There may be things families can do to support CBT.

✓ It is important to try not to let BDD take over family life; keep boundaries of what is acceptable and unacceptable, and try to keep as much as your life as normal.

✓ Make sure you have support for yourself in place; BDD is stressful for everyone.

8

WHAT CAN SCHOOLS AND PROFESSIONALS DO TO HELP?

This chapter will tell you:

- how schools can recognise there is a problem

- what can schools do to help

- what professionals can do to help.

How can schools recognise there is a problem?

You may have read Chapter 3 'The impact of BDD', which summarised how BDD can affect attendance and performance at school. It is helpful for teachers to look out for possible signs of BDD at school, which are in the box below.

POSSIBLE SIGNS OF BDD IN SCHOOLS

- Stepping out of class to check mirrors or other reflective surfaces

- Wearing excessive make-up or not adhering to uniform rules at school as a way of camouflaging appearance

- Being regularly late to school, inconsistent attendance or not attending at all

- Seeking reassurance about appearance

- Avoiding certain lessons such as PE where aspects of their appearance may be more visible

- Difficulty focusing in class due to appearance worries invading the student's mind

- Avoiding being around peers or groups

- Student becoming distressed or upset in class

- Decline in academic performance.

If you suspect a student may have BDD, it is helpful to explore this with the student or their family to facilitate them accessing support (see Chapter 7 'What can families, friends and carers do to help?').

What can schools do to help?

We know BDD is as common as other mental health difficulties; in fact, based on the available research, we know around 2% of the students in your school are likely to have this disorder. If you are aware of a student who has BDD, there are various ways you may be able to support them, as detailed in the box below.

TIPS ON HOW SCHOOLS CAN HELP

- Students may need time-out in lessons if they are feeling anxious or overwhelmed.

- They may need extra time to complete work in lessons or homework tasks.

- Avoid all comments on appearance – even positive comments – and don't discuss the perceived defect.

- Be aware that the student may be tired due to their appearance worries and the lengthy rituals they often engage in.

- Special adjustments may be needed to ensure the student is not disadvantaged (e.g. extra time in exams or taking exams in a smaller room).

- Be aware that students with BDD may experience difficulties with peer relationships and suffer low self-esteem. You may need to keep a lookout for any teasing and bullying of the student.

- It may be helpful to speak to the student to understand what are likely triggers and stressful aspects of school, and work together to come up with a plan to manage this (e.g. how can they discreetly signal if they need to leave the class?).

- If the student is having treatment, have regular contact with the family and/or therapist about specific provisions they will need in place to manage symptoms at school. It is helpful to ask about what they are working on in treatment and how the school can help.

- Learn more about BDD by visiting websites and reading books, and share this with other staff members (see 'Recommended reading, resources and organisations').

What can professionals do to help?

If you are a mental health professional, you may have a role in correctly identifying BDD as the diagnosis driving the young person's distress. BDD is sometimes just seen as normal appearance worries in teenagers, so their distress or concerns may be dismissed. Often young people with BDD are also embarrassed to admit their body image concerns for fear of appearing vain or drawing attention to their perceived flaw, so they struggle to disclose their concerns. As BDD may not be widely known about by professionals, it is commonly mistaken for other difficulties due to the overlap in symptoms, such as depression, social anxiety and eating disorders. It is important to explore BDD as a possible issue and to do so by directly asking the young person about appearance concerns. You can start by asking the simple questions in the box below.

QUESTIONS TO ASK A YOUNG PERSON IF YOU SUSPECT THEY HAVE BDD

1. Do you spend an hour or more every day worrying about your appearance?

2. Do you find yourself carrying out lots of behaviours (e.g. mirror checking, grooming) and/ or mental acts (e.g. comparing your appearance with other people's) in an effort to cope with your appearance worries?

3. Do your appearance worries make you feel miserable (e.g. anxious, depressed, ashamed) and/or get in the way of daily activities (e.g. socialising, going to school or leisure activities)?

4. Are your appearance concerns focused on being too fat or weighing too much?

If they answer 'yes' to questions 1–3 and 'no' to question 4, it is possible that they are experiencing BDD and you should support them to speak to a healthcare professional.

People with BDD have reported that they would not talk about their symptoms unless they were directly asked, due to shame or fear that people would think they were vain. Therefore, do not be afraid to ask the questions above while assuring them you do not think they are being vain or conceited. Do not get into conversations about aspects of their appearance; just ask the questions in a neutral and matter-of-fact way without giving opinions on their appearance. Do not challenge their perception of their appearance. It is important to remember that poor insight is very common in BDD. It is good to highlight that people are often concerned about multiple areas and often embarrassing areas, such as genitalia, in order to support the young person to disclose as much as they can. Keep the focus on the preoccupation, distress and interference this is causing them.

If the young person discloses that they are preoccupied by a perceived appearance concern which is slight or cannot be seen by others, and that they engage in behaviours which cause distress and interference in their lives, this is an indication that this is BDD. The ultimate goal of exploring this with the young person is to understand what may be driving their distress and facilitate them accessing support. If you are a mental health professional, you may wish to read Chapter 6 'Treatment for BDD' to guide you in offering and delivering an evidence-based treatment for BDD. It is important, as highlighted in Chapter 3 'The impact of BDD', that risk assessment and management are central to the support you offer, given that risk issues are common in BDD.

THINGS TO REMEMBER

✓ BDD can affect a young person's school life in a variety of ways and there are different ways students can be supported in this environment.

✓ It is important for the school and professionals to explore BDD as a possible explanation for the distress a young person may be experiencing and the impact this may be having on their life.

✓ When assessing BDD, avoid discussions about the perceived appearance 'defect' and focus on the distress the young person's concern is having on them.

✓ People with BDD often present with low mood, suicidal thoughts and self-harm behaviours. Make sure this is explored and that they have support in place for this.

Katie Holland

RECOMMENDED READING, RESOURCES AND ORGANISATIONS

Books

Claiborne, J. and Pedrick, C. (2002) *The BDD Workbook: Overcome Body Dysmorphic Disorder and End Body Image Obsessions*. Oakland, CA: New Harbinger Publications.

Clarke, A., Veale, D. and Willson, R. (2012) *Overcoming Body Image Problems Including Body Dysmorphic Disorder*. London: Hachette UK.

Phillips, K.A. (2005) *The Broken Mirror: Understanding and Treating Body Dysmorphic Disorder*. New York, NY: Oxford University Press.

Phillips, K. (2009) *Understanding Body Dysmorphic Disorder: An Essential Guide*. New York, NY: Oxford University Press.

Veale, D. and Neziroglu, F. (2010) *Body Dysmorphic Disorder: A Treatment Manual*. Chichester: Wiley-Blackwell.

Wilhelm, S. (2006) *Feeling Good about the Way You Look: A Program for Overcoming Body Image Problems*. New York, NY: The Guilford Press.

Wilhelm, S., Phillips, K.A. and Steketee, G. (2012) *Cognitive-Behavioral Therapy for Body Dysmorphic Disorder: A Treatment Manual*. New York, NY: The Guilford Press.

Organisations and websites

BDD Foundation – www.bddfoundation.org

OCD Action – www.ocdaction.org.uk

International OCD Foundation – https://iocdf.org

INDEX